Music Matters: The Profo
Melodies on our Everyday Experiences

Gerald Lori

Copyright © [2023]

Title: Music Matters: The Profound Effects of Melodies on our Everyday Experiences
Author's: Gerald Lori

This book was printed and published by [Publisher's: **Gerald Lori**] in [2023]

ISBN:

TABLE OF CONTENT

Chapter 7: Music and Social Interactions

44

Chapter 8: Music and Creativity

50

Chapter 9: Music and Education

56

Chapter 10: Conclusion: Harnessing the Power of Music in Everyday Life 62

Reflecting on the Profound Effects of Music

Practical Strategies for Integrating Music into Daily Routines

The Enduring Influence of Melodies on Our Everyday Experiences

Chapter 1: Introduction to the Power of Music

The Universal Language of Melodies

In the realm of human experiences, there exists a powerful force that transcends all barriers and connects us on a fundamental level - the language of melodies. No matter where we come from, our cultural background, or the language we speak, music has the ability to touch our souls and evoke profound emotions within us. Welcome to a chapter dedicated to exploring the universal language of melodies, where we delve into the reasons why music influences everything we do.

Music, in its various forms, has been an integral part of human existence since time immemorial. From ancient civilizations to modern societies, music has played a significant role in shaping our world and our individual lives. It has the power to inspire, heal, uplift, and even bring people together. But what is it about melodies that have such a profound effect on us?

One of the reasons music impacts us so deeply is its ability to tap into our emotions. When we listen to a melody that resonates with our current state of mind, it can intensify our feelings, whether it be joy, sadness, or nostalgia. It serves as a medium through which we can express and process our emotions, providing solace during difficult times and amplifying our happiness during moments of celebration.

Moreover, music has the unique ability to transcend language barriers. Regardless of whether we understand the lyrics or not, the melodies themselves can convey a vast range of emotions and messages. A melody can transport us to different places, evoke vivid imagery, and communicate complex ideas without the need for words. This universality of music allows it to reach people from different cultures and backgrounds, fostering a sense of unity and shared experience.

Additionally, music has a profound impact on our cognitive abilities. Numerous studies have shown that listening to music can enhance our focus, memory, and creativity. It has been used as a therapeutic tool to help individuals suffering from various conditions, including anxiety, depression, and neurological disorders. The harmonious vibrations of music have the power to heal and soothe our minds, providing a sanctuary in a chaotic world.

In conclusion, the universal language of melodies is a powerful force that influences every aspect of our lives. From the way it stirs our emotions to its ability to bring people together, music has the ability to touch our souls in ways that no other medium can. It transcends language barriers, enhances our cognitive abilities, and provides solace during challenging times. So next time you find yourself lost in a melody, remember the profound effects it has on our everyday experiences, and let it guide you on a journey of self-discovery and emotional connection.

Historical Significance of Music in Human Culture

Music has played an incredibly significant role in human culture throughout history. From ancient civilizations to modern societies, music has permeated every aspect of our lives. In this subchapter, we will explore the profound effects of melodies on our everyday experiences and why music influences everything we do.

The origins of music can be traced back to the earliest human civilizations. Archaeological evidence suggests that music was an integral part of rituals, ceremonies, and celebrations in ancient societies. For example, ancient Egyptians used music during religious ceremonies, while the Greeks incorporated music into their theatrical performances. These early cultures recognized the power of music to evoke emotions, create a sense of unity, and transcend language barriers.

Throughout the Middle Ages and the Renaissance, music continued to hold immense cultural significance. It was not only a form of entertainment but also a means of expressing religious devotion. Composers such as Bach, Mozart, and Beethoven composed masterpieces that still resonate with audiences today. The classical era saw the development of musical notation, enabling the preservation and dissemination of musical compositions.

As societies evolved and embraced technological advancements, music became more accessible to the masses. The invention of the phonograph and the radio allowed people to enjoy music in their homes, while the advent of the internet and digital music revolutionized the way we consume and share music. Today, music is just a click away, with streaming platforms providing a vast library of songs from various genres and cultures.

Music has the power to evoke powerful emotions and influence human behavior. It has been scientifically proven that listening to music can enhance our mood, reduce stress, and even improve cognitive function. It can transport us to different times and places, triggering memories and creating a sense of nostalgia. Music has the ability to bring people together, fostering a sense of community and shared experiences.

Moreover, music has always been intertwined with social and political movements, acting as a catalyst for change. From protest songs during the Civil Rights Movement to anti-war anthems during the Vietnam War, music has served as a platform for expressing dissent, spreading awareness, and inspiring social activism.

In conclusion, the historical significance of music in human culture cannot be overstated. It has shaped our rituals, inspired our creativity, and influenced our emotions. Whether it is a soothing melody, an energetic rhythm, or a thought-provoking lyric, music has the power to touch our souls and connect us with one another. It is a universal language that transcends borders and unites people from all walks of life. As we delve deeper into the profound effects of melodies on our everyday experiences, we will gain a greater appreciation for the role music plays in shaping our world.

The Purpose and Scope of this Book

Welcome to "Music Matters: The Profound Effects of Melodies on our Everyday Experiences." This book is dedicated to exploring the incredible impact that music has on every aspect of our lives. Whether you are a casual listener, a dedicated musician, or simply someone interested in the power of music, this book aims to uncover the reasons why music influences everything we do.

Why does a catchy tune get stuck in our heads? Why do we feel a surge of energy when our favorite song comes on? Why does music have the ability to evoke powerful emotions and transport us to different times and places? These are just a few of the questions we will delve into throughout the pages of this book.

The purpose of "Music Matters" is to shed light on the profound effects that melodies have on our everyday experiences. We will explore the science behind music and how it affects our brains, emotions, and even our physical well-being. This book aims to demystify the magic of music and provide insight into the mechanisms that make it such a universal language.

Moreover, this book is for everyone. Whether you are a music enthusiast, a psychologist, a teacher, a student, or simply someone who enjoys listening to their favorite tunes, "Music Matters" offers something for everyone. We believe that understanding the power of music can enhance our enjoyment and appreciation of it, and ultimately enrich our lives.

In this book, we will cover a wide range of topics. From the physiological effects of music on our bodies, to the psychological impact it has on our moods and behaviors, we will explore the many facets of music's influence. We will also delve into the cultural and historical significance of music, examining how it has shaped societies, rituals, and even political movements throughout history.

By the end of this book, we hope to have provided you with a comprehensive understanding of why music matters. We want to inspire you to listen more attentively, to appreciate the subtle nuances of melodies, and to explore the vast and diverse world of music.

So, join us on this captivating journey as we uncover the secrets of music and discover why it has the power to enhance, transform, and touch every aspect of our lives. Get ready to embrace the profound effects of music and unlock its hidden wonders. Let the melodies guide you as we embark on this fascinating exploration together.

Chapter 2: The Science Behind Music's Influence

How Music Affects the Brain

Music has a profound influence on our everyday experiences, shaping our thoughts, emotions, and actions in ways we may not even realize. Whether it's the catchy tune playing on the radio or the background music in a movie, music has a way of captivating our minds and souls. In this subchapter, we explore the fascinating ways in which music affects the brain and why it seems to permeate every aspect of our lives.

One of the most remarkable aspects of music is its ability to evoke emotions. Have you ever listened to a sad song and found tears welling up in your eyes? Or how about a catchy upbeat tune that instantly puts you in a good mood? These emotional responses are not coincidental but rather a result of the impact music has on our brain. Studies have shown that music activates various regions of the brain associated with emotions, such as the amygdala and hippocampus. This is why music can elicit such strong emotional reactions and even trigger memories from our past.

But the effects of music go beyond just emotions. Research has also demonstrated that music can enhance cognitive functions, such as memory and attention. When we listen to music, our brain releases dopamine, a neurotransmitter associated with pleasure and reward. This release of dopamine not only makes us feel good but also improves our ability to concentrate and retain information. In fact, many students find that listening to instrumental music while studying helps them focus and retain information more effectively.

Music also has the power to influence our behavior. Have you ever noticed how certain songs can make you want to dance or sing along? This is because music activates the motor cortex in our brain, which controls movement. It's no wonder that music is often used in exercise classes to motivate participants and enhance their performance.

In conclusion, music is a universal language that affects every aspect of our lives. It has the ability to evoke emotions, enhance cognitive functions, and influence our behavior. Whether we are consciously aware of it or not, music shapes our thoughts, feelings, and actions. So next time you find yourself humming along to a catchy tune, remember that it is not just a pleasant sound but a powerful force that has the potential to transform our everyday experiences.

The Role of Neurotransmitters in Musical Experiences

Have you ever wondered why music has such a profound impact on our everyday experiences? Why it has the power to uplift our mood, transport us back in time, or even bring tears to our eyes? The answer lies within the intricate workings of our brains and the role of neurotransmitters in shaping our musical encounters.

Neurotransmitters are chemical messengers in our brain that play a vital role in transmitting signals between nerve cells. They are responsible for regulating various functions, including mood, emotions, and cognition. When it comes to music, these neurotransmitters are at the heart of how melodies influence our thoughts and behaviors.

One of the key neurotransmitters involved in musical experiences is dopamine. Known as the "feel-good" neurotransmitter, dopamine is released in response to pleasurable stimuli, such as delicious food, romantic encounters, and yes, you guessed it, music. When we listen to music that resonates with us, dopamine floods our brain, creating a sense of euphoria and reward. This explains why music has the power to enhance our mood and provide us with a natural high.

Another neurotransmitter at play is serotonin, often referred to as the "happiness hormone." Serotonin helps regulate our mood, sleep, and appetite. Studies have shown that listening to music increases serotonin levels in the brain, leading to a sense of calmness, relaxation, and overall well-being. This is why many people turn to music as a form of therapy during times of stress or anxiety.

Furthermore, music has been found to stimulate the release of endorphins, our body's natural painkillers. These neurotransmitters not only reduce pain but also create feelings of pleasure and euphoria. So, the next time you find yourself dancing to your favorite tune, remember that the release of endorphins is contributing to that incredible sense of joy and freedom.

Understanding the role of neurotransmitters in musical experiences helps us appreciate the profound effects that melodies have on our daily lives. Whether it's boosting our mood, reducing stress, or simply providing a momentary escape, music has the power to enhance every aspect of our existence. So, the next time you find yourself tapping your feet or singing along to a catchy tune, embrace the magical interplay between your brain and those delightful neurotransmitters. Music truly matters, as it influences everything we do.

Emotional Responses to Different Types of Music

Music has an astonishing power to touch our emotions and influence our moods. It is a universal language that can transcend cultural barriers and connect people on a deeply emotional level. Whether we are aware of it or not, music affects us in various ways, and different types of music can elicit distinct emotional responses within us.

When we listen to upbeat and lively music, such as pop or dance tunes, our bodies naturally start moving to the rhythm. These energetic beats have the ability to uplift our spirits, make us feel more joyful, and even ignite a sense of euphoria. We find ourselves tapping our feet, nodding our heads, or even breaking into dance. This type of music can be a powerful tool to boost our energy levels and motivate us during physical activities or mundane tasks.

On the other hand, there are also slower, more melancholic tunes that evoke a range of emotions. Ballads or classical compositions can evoke feelings of sadness, nostalgia, or introspection. These types of music often accompany moments of reflection or solitude, allowing us to delve into our thoughts and emotions. They can provide solace during times of heartbreak or help us process complex feelings.

Aside from these extremes, different genres of music can elicit a wide variety of emotions. For example, heavy metal or hard rock may provoke a sense of empowerment, anger, or rebellion, while jazz or blues can evoke a feeling of relaxation or introspection. The lyrics of a song can further enhance or alter our emotions, as they communicate specific messages or narratives that resonate with our own experiences.

Music's ability to alter our emotional states is not only limited to listening. Playing an instrument or singing can also have a profound impact on our well-being. Engaging in music-making activities has been shown to reduce stress and anxiety, increase self-confidence, and foster a sense of accomplishment.

In conclusion, music has a profound effect on our emotional lives. It has the power to uplift, comfort, and inspire us. Whether we are consciously aware of it or not, different types of music can evoke a wide range of emotions within us, from joy and excitement to sadness and contemplation. Understanding how music influences our emotions can help us harness its power and use it to enhance our everyday experiences.

"Music Matters: The Profound Effects of Melodies on our Everyday Experiences" delves further into this fascinating realm, exploring the science behind our emotional responses to music and providing practical insights on how to harness its power in various aspects of our lives.

Chapter 3: Music as a Mood Enhancer

The Impact of Music on Emotional Well-being

Music has an incredible power to influence our emotions and shape our well-being in profound ways. From the moment we are born, we are surrounded by music, and this constant presence has a significant impact on our daily lives. In this subchapter, we will explore the various ways in which music affects our emotional well-being.

One of the most remarkable aspects of music is its ability to evoke emotions. Whether it's a joyful melody that uplifts our spirits or a melancholic tune that brings tears to our eyes, music has the power to elicit strong emotional responses. Scientific studies have shown that listening to music can stimulate the release of neurotransmitters such as dopamine, serotonin, and oxytocin, which are responsible for feelings of pleasure, happiness, and bonding. This explains why certain songs can instantly improve our mood and create a sense of connection with others.

Moreover, music has the ability to act as a therapeutic tool for managing and regulating emotions. Many individuals turn to music as a form of self-expression and catharsis during difficult times. Whether it's playing an instrument, singing, or simply listening, music provides a safe outlet for expressing and processing emotions. Research has shown that engaging with music can reduce stress, anxiety, and depression, as well as enhance feelings of relaxation and overall well-being.

In addition to its immediate effects, music also has long-term benefits for emotional well-being. Learning to play an instrument or engaging in musical activities from a young age can have a lasting impact on brain development and emotional intelligence. Studies have demonstrated that children who receive musical training exhibit better emotional regulation, higher empathy levels, and improved social skills compared to their non-musical peers. These skills continue to benefit individuals throughout their lives, helping them navigate complex emotional landscapes and maintain positive mental health.

Furthermore, music has the power to enhance our everyday experiences, whether it's providing a soundtrack to our daily routines or intensifying the emotions we feel during significant life events. Think about how music is intricately woven into movies, commercials, and even sporting events. It has the ability to heighten our emotions, create a sense of anticipation, and evoke powerful memories. From celebrating achievements to comforting us in times of sorrow, music accompanies us through every aspect of our lives.

In conclusion, music plays an integral role in shaping our emotional well-being. It has the power to evoke and regulate emotions, enhance our daily experiences, and even contribute to our long-term emotional intelligence. Whether we are consciously aware of it or not, music influences every aspect of our lives, making it an essential component of our existence. So, let us embrace the profound effects of melodies and allow music to continue enriching and impacting our emotional well-being.

Using Music to Reduce Stress and Anxiety

In our fast-paced and often overwhelming modern world, stress and anxiety have become all too common. The constant pressure to perform, meet deadlines, and juggle multiple responsibilities can take a toll on our mental and physical well-being. Fortunately, there is a powerful tool that can help alleviate these burdens and restore a sense of calm and serenity – music.

Music has a profound impact on our everyday experiences, and its ability to reduce stress and anxiety should not be underestimated. Research has shown that listening to music can have a direct physiological effect on our bodies, such as lowering blood pressure and heart rate. Additionally, it can stimulate the release of endorphins, which are natural mood enhancers. These effects combine to create a soothing and therapeutic experience for the listener.

One of the reasons why music has such a profound impact on our stress levels is its ability to tap into our emotions. Different genres and melodies have the power to evoke specific emotions, whether it be happiness, sadness, or relaxation. By consciously choosing music that promotes relaxation, we can actively reduce stress and anxiety. Classical music, for example, has been found to have particularly calming effects on the mind and body.

Furthermore, music can serve as a distraction from our worries and negative thoughts. When we immerse ourselves in a piece of music, our attention is diverted from the stressors of our daily lives. This shift in focus allows our minds to relax and find solace in the melodies. Whether it's through actively listening to music or using it as background noise, this diversion can provide a much-needed break from the pressures of life.

In addition to listening, actively engaging with music through activities such as singing, playing an instrument, or dancing can also reduce stress and anxiety. These activities release pent-up emotions and tension, helping to alleviate the burden on our minds and bodies. Music can serve as a form of self-expression, allowing us to let go of our worries and connect with our inner selves.

In conclusion, music has the incredible power to reduce stress and anxiety in our lives. By consciously choosing calming melodies, immersing ourselves in music, and actively engaging with it, we can harness its therapeutic effects. So, the next time you feel overwhelmed, take a moment to indulge in the power of music – it may just be the remedy you need to find peace and tranquility in your everyday life.

Music's Role in Boosting Mood and Energy Levels

Music has an extraordinary ability to influence our emotions and energy levels, making it an essential part of our everyday experiences. Whether we are aware of it or not, music has the power to shape our moods, lift our spirits, and invigorate our bodies. In this subchapter, we will explore how music affects our mood and energy levels and why it plays such a significant role in our lives.

Have you ever noticed how a particular song can instantly change your mood? The moment you hear a catchy tune or a familiar melody, your brain lights up, and you can't help but tap your feet or sing along. This is because music activates the pleasure centers in our brains, releasing dopamine, a feel-good neurotransmitter. As a result, our mood is instantly lifted, and we feel a surge of positive emotions.

Furthermore, music has the remarkable ability to evoke memories and transport us back to specific moments in our lives. A certain song can remind us of a cherished memory or an exhilarating experience, instantly boosting our mood and bringing a smile to our faces. This connection between music, memories, and emotions is a powerful tool that we can utilize to enhance our overall well-being.

In addition to its impact on our mood, music also has the power to energize us. Have you ever noticed how the right beat or rhythm can make you feel more motivated and energetic? Upbeat and fast-paced music has been proven to increase heart rate and stimulate physical movement. Whether you are hitting the gym, going for a run, or simply need an energy boost throughout the day, music can be your ideal companion.

Moreover, music can also improve our focus and productivity. Many people find that listening to music while working or studying helps them concentrate and enhances their cognitive performance. The right background music can drown out distractions and create a conducive environment for deep focus and creative thinking.

In conclusion, music plays an integral role in boosting our mood and energy levels. Its ability to evoke emotions, trigger memories, and stimulate physical movement makes it an essential part of our everyday experiences. Whether we need an instant mood lift, an energy boost, or improved focus, music can always come to our rescue. So, next time you feel down or need a pick-me-up, put on your favorite tunes and let the melodies work their magic on your mind, body, and soul.

Chapter 4: Music and Productivity

The Connection Between Music and Focus

In today's fast-paced and ever-distracting world, maintaining focus has become an essential skill. Whether you are a student studying for exams, an employee trying to meet deadlines, or simply someone trying to complete daily tasks efficiently, the ability to concentrate is crucial. Interestingly, one tool that has been found to significantly enhance focus is music.

Music has a profound effect on our everyday experiences, and it goes beyond mere enjoyment or entertainment. Numerous studies have shown that listening to music can improve concentration, memory, and overall cognitive performance. It has the power to engage our brains and create a state of flow, where we become fully absorbed in the task at hand.

But how does music accomplish this? The key lies in its ability to activate multiple areas of the brain simultaneously. When we listen to music, various regions responsible for processing sound, emotions, and movement are all stimulated. This activation enhances our cognitive functions and primes us for heightened focus.

The type of music we choose to listen to also plays a significant role. While personal preferences may vary, certain genres have been found to be particularly effective in promoting concentration. Classical music, for instance, is known for its calming and soothing effect on the mind. Its complex and structured compositions have been shown to increase focus, especially when engaged in activities that require sustained attention.

Ambient and instrumental music are also highly recommended for enhancing concentration. These genres lack lyrics, eliminating any potential distractions caused by trying to process the words. Their gentle melodies and repetitive patterns create a soothing background that can help drown out external noise and keep our minds centered on the task at hand.

Moreover, music can serve as a powerful psychological tool to enhance focus. By creating a designated playlist for specific activities, such as studying or working, we can condition our brains to associate that music with concentration. This conditioning helps us enter a focused state more easily whenever we hear those familiar tunes.

In conclusion, the connection between music and focus is undeniable. Incorporating music into our daily routines can have a profound impact on our ability to concentrate and perform tasks efficiently. Understanding the power of music and harnessing its potential can transform the way we approach our everyday lives. So, next time you find yourself struggling to stay focused, plug in your headphones and let the melodies guide you to a state of enhanced productivity.

Utilizing Music for Enhanced Concentration

In today's fast-paced world, it can be challenging to maintain focus and concentration amidst a multitude of distractions. This is where the power of music comes into play. Music has the remarkable ability to enhance our concentration levels and improve productivity in various aspects of our lives. Whether it's studying for an exam, working on a project, or even engaging in physical exercise, the right music can significantly impact our performance and overall experience.

Music has a profound effect on our brain, altering our mood, emotions, and cognitive functions. Numerous studies have shown that certain types of music can promote a state of relaxation and focus, allowing us to dive deeper into our tasks. The rhythmic patterns, melodies, and harmonies found in music stimulate the release of dopamine, a neurotransmitter associated with pleasure and reward. As a result, music can enhance our motivation and engagement, leading to improved concentration and productivity.

When it comes to selecting the right music for enhanced concentration, individual preferences play a crucial role. While some people find classical music to be ideal for focus and concentration, others may find instrumental or ambient music more suitable. It is essential to experiment and discover which genre or style best suits your personal taste and helps you enter a state of flow.

Moreover, the tempo, or speed, of the music can also influence our concentration levels. Fast-paced music with a higher tempo may be beneficial for tasks that require quick thinking and creativity, while slower tempos can promote a calm and relaxed state of mind, ideal for studying or reading. Experimenting with different tempos and genres can help you identify the music that works best for you in different scenarios.

In addition to aiding concentration, music can also help block out external distractions. By creating a sonic environment, music can mask background noises and create a sense of privacy, allowing you to focus solely on the task at hand. This is particularly useful in busy environments such as open offices or public spaces, where external sounds can be disruptive.

In conclusion, music plays an integral role in enhancing concentration in various aspects of our lives. By understanding our personal preferences and experimenting with different genres and tempos, we can harness the power of music to improve our productivity, engagement, and overall well-being. So, the next time you find yourself struggling to concentrate, put on some tunes and let the melodies guide you into a state of enhanced focus and efficiency.

Music's Effect on Work Performance and Efficiency

Introduction:

Music has always been a powerful force in our lives, capable of evoking emotions, memories, and even physical responses. But did you know that music also has a profound impact on our work performance and efficiency? In this subchapter of "Music Matters: The Profound Effects of Melodies on our Everyday Experiences," we will explore how music affects our productivity, focus, and overall effectiveness in various work environments.

Enhancing Focus and Concentration:

Have you ever found yourself struggling to concentrate on a task at hand? It turns out that music can be a potent tool to help improve focus and concentration. Numerous studies have shown that certain types of music, such as classical or instrumental tunes, can help create a conducive atmosphere for deep work. By blocking out distractions and providing a soothing backdrop, music can enable us to enter a state of flow, where productivity and creativity thrive.

Boosting Mood and Motivation:

Have you ever noticed how listening to your favorite upbeat song instantly lifts your mood and motivates you to tackle even the most challenging tasks? Music has a direct impact on our emotions, and by choosing the right tunes, we can harness its power to enhance our work performance. Upbeat and energetic music releases dopamine in our brains, a neurotransmitter associated with pleasure and reward.

This surge of positive emotions can help us overcome procrastination, increase motivation, and ultimately improve our efficiency at work.

Reducing Stress and Anxiety:

In today's fast-paced world, stress and anxiety have become common companions in the workplace. However, music can act as a powerful stress reliever. Slow, melodic tunes or ambient sounds can help calm our nervous system, reducing stress levels and promoting relaxation. By incorporating soothing music into our work routine, we can create a more tranquil environment, leading to improved mental clarity and better decision-making abilities.

Enhancing Creativity and Problem-Solving Skills:

Have you ever noticed how some of your best ideas come to you while listening to music? Research suggests that music stimulates both hemispheres of our brain, enhancing our creative thinking and problem-solving abilities. The right music can help us think outside the box, connect seemingly unrelated concepts, and approach challenges with a fresh perspective. By tapping into our creative potential, music can significantly boost our work performance and efficiency.

Conclusion:

Music's effect on work performance and efficiency is undeniable. Whether we need to focus, boost our mood, reduce stress, or enhance our creativity, music can be a valuable tool in our arsenal. By understanding how different types of music affect us, we can harness its power to optimize our work environments and reach new heights of productivity. So, the next time you find yourself needing a productivity boost, don't forget to press play on your favorite tunes and let the melodies work their magic.

Chapter 5: Music and Memory

Music's Ability to Trigger Memories

In our daily lives, music has an uncanny ability to evoke emotions, transport us to different times and places, and most notably, trigger memories. Whether it's a favorite song from our teenage years or a tune associated with a significant life event, music has a profound impact on our ability to recall memories and relive the moments that are etched in our minds.

The connection between music and memory is a fascinating phenomenon that has captivated researchers and music enthusiasts alike. Numerous studies have explored the relationship between music and memory, revealing the powerful influence that melodies can have on our ability to remember past experiences. It is a universal phenomenon that transcends cultural, social, and linguistic barriers, making it relevant to people from all walks of life.

When we hear a familiar song, the brain's hippocampus, responsible for memory formation and retrieval, is activated. This activation triggers a flood of memories associated with the song, bringing back vivid images, emotions, and even physical sensations. It is as if music has the power to unlock the doors to our past, allowing us to re-experience moments that would otherwise remain dormant.

The memories triggered by music are not limited to major life events or milestones. Even the most mundane activities can be enhanced by the right musical accompaniment. For instance, listening to a specific genre of music while cooking dinner can transport us back to family gatherings or remind us of cherished moments spent in the kitchen with loved ones. Similarly, hearing a song while exercising can bring back memories of past workouts, motivating us to push our limits and achieve our fitness goals.

Furthermore, music's ability to trigger memories extends to individuals with cognitive impairments, such as Alzheimer's disease or dementia. Even when other memories have faded, music can still evoke powerful emotions and awaken dormant memories in these individuals. This phenomenon has led to the development of music therapy programs, which utilize music as a therapeutic tool to improve cognitive function and enhance the quality of life for those living with memory-related disorders.

In conclusion, music's ability to trigger memories is a universal phenomenon that impacts every one of us. Whether it's reliving past experiences, enhancing everyday activities, or aiding those with cognitive impairments, the profound effects of melodies on our everyday experiences cannot be underestimated. So, the next time you find yourself humming along to a familiar tune, embrace the memories that flood your mind and appreciate the power that music holds in connecting us to our past.

Using Music as a Memory Aid

In our daily lives, we encounter numerous situations where we struggle to remember important information. Whether it is remembering someone's name, a phone number, or a shopping list, our memory often fails us. However, did you know that music can be a powerful tool to enhance our memory and improve our ability to recall information? In this subchapter, we will explore the fascinating phenomenon of using music as a memory aid.

Music has a profound effect on our everyday experiences, and it seems to have a unique way of ingraining itself into our minds. Have you ever noticed how a particular song can instantly transport you back in time, evoking vivid memories and emotions? This is because music activates various regions of our brain, including those responsible for memory formation and emotional processing.

Research suggests that music can enhance our memory in several ways. First and foremost, music helps us establish strong associations between information and melodies. By linking new information to a catchy tune, we create a powerful mnemonic device that aids in memory retrieval. Think about how you learned the ABC song as a child – the melody helped you remember the order of the letters effortlessly.

Furthermore, music activates the brain's reward system, releasing dopamine, a neurotransmitter associated with pleasure and motivation. This release of dopamine can enhance our focus and attention, making it easier to encode and remember information. So, the next time you are studying for an exam or trying to learn a new skill, consider adding some background music to your study sessions.

Interestingly, research has also shown that listening to familiar music can be particularly effective in stimulating memory retrieval. This is because our brains create strong connections between music and memories, especially those associated with significant events or emotions. So, if you are trying to recall a specific memory, try listening to the songs that were playing during that period. It might surprise you how effortlessly the memories come flooding back.

In conclusion, music has a profound impact on our memory and can be used as a powerful tool to aid in memory recall. By establishing associations between melodies and information, activating the brain's reward system, and leveraging the connections between music and memories, we can enhance our ability to remember important information. So, the next time you find yourself struggling to remember something, turn to music as your memory aid and unlock the profound effects melodies can have on our everyday experiences.

Music Therapy for Memory Improvement

Memory is an integral aspect of our daily lives, enabling us to recall past experiences, learn new information, and navigate the world around us. However, as we age, memory decline becomes a common concern for many individuals. Fortunately, the power of music can be harnessed as an effective tool in improving memory and cognitive function. This subchapter explores the fascinating realm of music therapy for memory improvement and how melodies can positively impact our everyday experiences.

Music has a unique ability to evoke emotions, trigger memories, and stimulate various areas of the brain. When we listen to music, our brains become engaged in a complex network of neural connections, enhancing our cognitive processing. Studies have shown that music therapy can significantly improve memory function in individuals with dementia, Alzheimer's disease, and other age-related cognitive disorders. The rhythmic patterns, melodies, and harmonies in music activate the brain's memory centers, facilitating the retrieval of stored information and improving overall cognitive performance.

In addition to its therapeutic benefits for individuals with cognitive impairments, music therapy can also be beneficial for everyone, regardless of age or background. Listening to music while studying or engaging in mentally demanding tasks can enhance concentration, focus, and memory retention. The repetitive and predictable nature of music aids in the encoding and storage of information, making it easier to recall later on.

Furthermore, actively engaging in music-making, such as playing an instrument or singing, can have profound effects on memory improvement. Learning to play an instrument requires coordination, concentration, and memory recall, strengthening neural connections and promoting overall brain health. Studies have shown that musicians have enhanced memory skills compared to non-musicians, highlighting the long-term benefits of musical engagement.

Music therapy for memory improvement is not limited to specific genres or styles. Different types of music can evoke different emotions and stimulate various brain regions. Classical music, for example, is known to enhance focus and relaxation, making it ideal for studying or engaging in creative tasks. On the other hand, upbeat and energetic music can boost mood and motivation, making it an excellent choice for physical exercise or mundane activities.

In conclusion, music therapy has the potential to significantly improve memory and cognitive function for individuals of all ages and backgrounds. Whether it's passively listening to music, actively engaging in music-making, or incorporating music into daily activities, melodies have profound effects on our everyday experiences. By harnessing the power of music, we can enhance our memory, cognitive abilities, and overall well-being. So, why not let music permeate everything we do and unlock the incredible benefits it offers?

Chapter 6: Music and Physical Health

The Physiological Effects of Music on the Body

In the fast-paced world we live in, music has become an integral part of our everyday experiences. Whether we are driving, working out, or simply relaxing at home, music has the power to enhance our moods and transport us to different emotional landscapes. But have you ever wondered why music seems to have such a profound effect on our bodies? In this subchapter, we will explore the physiological effects of music and uncover the fascinating ways it influences our physical well-being.

From the moment we hear a catchy beat or a soothing melody, our bodies undergo a series of physiological changes. Research has shown that listening to music can trigger the release of dopamine, a neurotransmitter associated with pleasure and reward. This surge of dopamine not only uplifts our mood but also boosts our motivation and cognitive function. That's why many people find that listening to music while working or studying helps them stay focused and productive.

Moreover, music has the remarkable ability to influence our heart rate and blood pressure. Upbeat and fast-paced music tends to increase our heart rate, while slow and calming tunes have the opposite effect, promoting relaxation and reducing stress. This physiological response can be attributed to the activation of the autonomic nervous system, which regulates our body's involuntary functions. By understanding how different types of music affect our heart rate and blood pressure, we can better utilize music as a tool for stress management and overall well-being.

But the physiological effects of music go beyond just our hearts. Research has also demonstrated that music can have a significant impact on our immune system. Studies have found that listening to music, especially classical compositions, can increase the production of antibodies and enhance the activity of natural killer cells, which are crucial for fighting off infections and diseases. This suggests that incorporating music into our daily routines can potentially strengthen our immune system and improve our overall health.

In conclusion, music possesses tremendous power over our bodies. Its ability to release dopamine, influence our heart rate and blood pressure, and even boost our immune system showcases the profound effects melodies have on our everyday experiences. Whether you are seeking motivation, relaxation, or a way to enhance your physical well-being, music has the potential to provide the perfect soundtrack to every aspect of your life. So, the next time you find yourself tapping your foot to a catchy tune, remember that music truly does matter, and it affects every single thing we do.

Music's Impact on Exercise Performance

Subchapter: Music's Impact on Exercise Performance

Introduction:
In this subchapter, we delve into the profound effects of music on our exercise performance. Music has the power to elevate our mood, increase motivation, and even enhance physical endurance during workouts. Whether you're a fitness enthusiast or a casual exerciser, understanding the impact of music on your exercise routine can revolutionize your fitness journey.

The   Power   of   Music:
Music has an incredible ability to influence our emotions and energy levels. When we listen to music we enjoy, our brain releases dopamine, a neurotransmitter associated with pleasure and reward. This surge of dopamine not only enhances our mood but also stimulates motivation and focus, making exercise feel more enjoyable and less strenuous.

Increase   in   Performance:
Studies have shown that listening to upbeat and motivational music during exercise can significantly improve performance. The right tempo and rhythm can synchronize with our movements, enabling us to maintain a steady pace and optimize our energy expenditure. Additionally, music can distract us from feelings of fatigue, allowing us to push through physical barriers and achieve higher levels of endurance.

Enhanced   Focus   and   Productivity:
Music can also enhance our focus and productivity during exercise. The right kind of music can drown out external distractions, helping

us stay in the zone and concentrate on our workout. This increased focus allows us to perform exercises with better form and technique, reducing the risk of injury and maximizing the effectiveness of our workouts.

Personalization and Individual Preferences: One of the most exciting aspects of incorporating music into exercise is the ability to personalize your workout playlist. Everyone has unique musical preferences, and finding the right genre, tempo, and lyrics can make a world of difference in your performance. Whether it's upbeat pop music, energizing rock anthems, or soothing classical melodies, the music you choose should align with your personal taste and exercise goals.

Conclusion:
The impact of music on exercise performance cannot be overstated. From boosting mood and motivation to enhancing endurance and focus, music has the power to elevate our fitness experiences. Whether you're hitting the gym, going for a run, or engaging in any other form of physical activity, don't underestimate the potential benefits of incorporating music into your routine. So, put on your headphones, create a playlist that speaks to you, and let the melodies propel you towards your fitness goals. Remember, with the right music, anything is possible.

Music's Role in Pain Management and Recovery

Music has always been a powerful medium that has the ability to touch our souls and evoke a wide range of emotions. It is no surprise then that music can also play a significant role in managing pain and aiding in the process of recovery. In this subchapter, we explore the profound effects of melodies on our everyday experiences, specifically focusing on how music can alleviate pain and promote healing.

Pain is an inevitable aspect of human existence, and finding effective ways to manage it is crucial for our overall well-being. Traditional methods such as medication and therapy have long been relied upon, but music offers a unique and complementary approach that can enhance the healing process. Numerous studies have demonstrated the positive impact of music on pain management, showing that it can reduce the perception of pain, decrease anxiety levels, and even lower the need for pain medication.

One of the key reasons behind music's effectiveness in pain management lies in its ability to divert our attention away from the discomfort we are experiencing. When we immerse ourselves in music, our focus shifts, and we become engrossed in the rhythms, melodies, and lyrics. This diversionary effect can significantly reduce the intensity of pain we feel, making it more manageable.

Furthermore, music has the power to evoke emotions and trigger the release of endorphins, our body's natural painkillers. By listening to music that resonates with us personally, we tap into a world of emotions that can positively influence our pain experience. Upbeat and uplifting melodies can boost our mood, providing a much-needed distraction from pain and promoting a sense of well-being.

In addition to pain management, music also plays a crucial role in the process of recovery. Whether it's physical rehabilitation or emotional healing, music can provide a supportive and motivating environment. By incorporating music into therapy sessions or exercise routines, individuals can experience increased motivation, improved motor coordination, and enhanced emotional expression.

Furthermore, music has the ability to trigger memories and emotions associated with different periods of our lives. This can be particularly beneficial for individuals who are recovering from trauma or undergoing emotional healing. By using music as a therapeutic tool, individuals can explore their feelings and memories, ultimately facilitating their recovery journey.

In conclusion, music has a profound impact on our everyday experiences, and its role in pain management and recovery is undeniable. From reducing pain perception to promoting healing and emotional expression, music offers a unique and powerful approach to managing pain and supporting the recovery process. Incorporating music into our lives can truly transform our experiences, making it an essential element in our journey towards holistic well-being.

Chapter 7: Music and Social Interactions

Music's Influence on Social Bonding

In today's fast-paced world, where technology dominates our interactions, music stands as a timeless and powerful force that brings people together. Whether it's in the form of a catchy tune, a melodic harmony, or a rhythmic beat, music has a profound impact on our lives, and more specifically, on our social bonding.

Music has the extraordinary ability to transcend cultural, linguistic, and even generational barriers. It is a universal language that speaks to the core of our emotions, creating a shared experience that unites individuals from diverse backgrounds. Whether we're attending a concert, singing along with friends, or dancing at a party, music cultivates a sense of community and fosters connections that go beyond superficial interactions.

The power of music in social bonding can be witnessed in various settings. For instance, think about how often you find yourself singing along to your favorite song with friends or family. It's a simple act that instantly creates a sense of camaraderie and belonging. In these moments, music acts as a catalyst for shared experiences and strengthens the bond between individuals.

Furthermore, music has the ability to enhance group cohesion and cooperation. Research has shown that when people engage in synchronized activities such as singing or dancing together, their sense of unity and cooperation increases. This phenomenon can be observed in various cultural practices, such as tribal drumming or community singing, where music plays a vital role in fostering a sense of togetherness and cooperation.

Moreover, music can also facilitate self-expression and emotional connection, leading to deeper social connections. When we share our favorite songs or discuss the emotional impact of a particular melody, we invite others into our inner world, allowing them to understand us better. Through music, we can communicate our thoughts, feelings, and experiences in a way that words alone often fail to convey, forging bonds based on empathy and understanding.

In conclusion, music's influence on social bonding is undeniable. It has the power to break down barriers, create a sense of community, enhance cooperation, and foster emotional connections. Whether it's through singing, dancing, or simply sharing our favorite tunes, music brings people together, reminding us of the common thread that unites humanity. So, next time you find yourself tapping your feet to the rhythm or belting out a song with friends, remember that music is not just a form of entertainment; it's a powerful force that has the potential to transform our relationships and enrich our everyday experiences.

Music's Role in Cultural Identity and Community

Music has always played a powerful role in shaping our cultural identity and fostering a sense of community. It has the unique ability to transcend language barriers, unite diverse groups of people, and evoke deep emotions. Whether it is through traditional folk songs, national anthems, or contemporary popular music, melodies have the profound ability to reflect the values, beliefs, and history of a particular culture.

One of the most significant ways in which music contributes to cultural identity is by preserving and transmitting traditions from one generation to the next. Through the ages, songs have been passed down orally, carrying stories, rituals, and important social messages. They serve as a living record of a community's history, struggles, and triumphs. By preserving these musical traditions, communities can maintain a connection to their roots and cultural heritage.

Music also acts as a powerful tool for social cohesion and community building. It brings people together, encourages collaboration, and promotes a sense of belonging. Whether it is singing in a choir, participating in a drum circle, or attending a live concert, music has the ability to break down barriers and create a shared experience. It allows individuals to connect with one another on a deeper level, foster empathy, and build stronger relationships.

Furthermore, music has the remarkable ability to evoke emotions and influence our everyday experiences. It can uplift our spirits, provide solace during challenging times, and even motivate us to take action. From the joyous celebrations of weddings and festivals to the solemn rituals of mourning, music accompanies us through life's most significant moments, shaping our perceptions and enhancing our overall well-being.

In today's fast-paced and interconnected world, music continues to play an essential role. It has the power to bridge gaps between cultures, promote understanding, and encourage dialogue. The global popularity of genres like hip-hop, reggae, and K-pop demonstrates the universal appeal of music and its ability to transcend geographical boundaries.

In conclusion, music's role in cultural identity and community cannot be overstated. It serves as a powerful tool for preserving traditions, fostering a sense of belonging, and influencing our emotions and experiences. Whether you are singing along to your favorite song, attending a concert, or exploring the musical traditions of a different culture, remember the profound effects melodies have on our everyday lives. Embrace the power of music and let it enrich your cultural identity and community.

Using Music to Enhance Social Gatherings and Events

Music has a profound impact on our everyday experiences, and its ability to enhance social gatherings and events is undeniable. Whether it's a small get-together with friends or a large-scale celebration, music has the power to create an atmosphere that brings people together, sets the mood, and leaves a lasting impression.

One of the primary reasons why music influences everything we do is its ability to evoke emotions. The right melody can instantly uplift our spirits, make us feel nostalgic, or even bring tears to our eyes. When incorporated into social gatherings and events, music has the magical ability to amplify these emotions and create a deeper connection among the attendees. It sets the tone for the occasion, be it a joyful celebration or a solemn gathering.

Moreover, music acts as a universal language that transcends cultural and linguistic barriers. It has the power to unite people from different backgrounds, allowing them to share a common experience and form connections. Whether it's a lively dance tune or a soulful ballad, music can bring individuals together, encouraging them to let loose, have fun, and embrace the moment.

Incorporating music into social gatherings and events also helps to create a sense of identity and belonging. A carefully curated playlist that reflects the tastes and preferences of the attendees can make them feel seen and understood. It adds a personal touch to the occasion and enhances the overall experience, making people feel more engaged and invested in the event.

Furthermore, music has the ability to stimulate social interaction and encourage participation. Whether it's singing along to a favorite song, dancing together, or even playing musical instruments, music provides a common activity that encourages people to engage with one another. It breaks down barriers and fosters a sense of camaraderie, allowing individuals to bond and create lasting memories.

In conclusion, music plays an integral role in enhancing social gatherings and events. Its ability to evoke emotions, unite people, create a sense of identity, and encourage interaction makes it an indispensable tool for event organizers and hosts. By understanding the profound effects of melodies on our everyday experiences, we can harness the power of music to create unforgettable moments and foster stronger connections among individuals from all walks of life. So, the next time you're planning a social gathering or event, remember to let music take center stage and watch as it transforms the occasion into something truly remarkable.

Chapter 8: Music and Creativity

How Music Inspires Creative Thinking

In our fast-paced world, where creativity is highly valued, finding effective ways to enhance our creative thinking is crucial. Surprisingly, one of the most powerful tools we have at our disposal is music. Music has the ability to reach deep into our souls, evoking emotions and memories that can fuel our creative processes. In this subchapter, we will explore how music inspires creative thinking and why it has the profound effect of influencing every aspect of our lives.

Music has been intertwined with human culture for centuries, and its impact on our daily experiences is undeniable. Whether we are consciously aware of it or not, music has a way of influencing our moods, thoughts, and actions. When we listen to music that resonates with us, it can transport us to different places, unlock our imagination, and ignite our creative spark.

Studies have shown that listening to music stimulates the release of dopamine, a neurotransmitter associated with pleasure and reward. This surge of dopamine not only enhances our mood but also boosts our cognitive abilities, including creative thinking. By engaging different areas of our brain simultaneously, music has the power to enhance our problem-solving skills and inspire innovative ideas.

Furthermore, music has the unique ability to bypass our rational thinking and tap into our subconscious mind. It can evoke emotions and memories that we may have long forgotten, providing a rich source of inspiration for our creative endeavors. Whether we are writers, painters, or entrepreneurs, music can serve as a catalyst for exploring new ideas and approaching challenges from a fresh perspective.

Moreover, music has the incredible power to create a sense of flow, a state of complete immersion and focus in an activity. When we are in this state, our creative juices flow effortlessly, and we become fully absorbed in the task at hand. By choosing the right music that resonates with our personal preferences, we can create an optimal environment for creative thinking to flourish.

In conclusion, music truly matters when it comes to enhancing our creative thinking. Its ability to evoke emotions, stimulate our brains, and create a state of flow makes it an invaluable tool for anyone seeking to unleash their creative potential. By incorporating music into our everyday lives, we can tap into its profound effects and unlock a world of inspiration that can revolutionize every aspect of what we do. So, let the melodies guide you and watch as your creativity soars to new heights.

Music's Role in Artistic Expression and Innovation

Music has always been an integral part of human civilization, transcending cultural boundaries and connecting people on a universal level. It has the power to evoke emotions, ignite memories, and inspire creativity. In this subchapter, we delve into the profound effects of melodies on our everyday experiences, exploring how music serves as a catalyst for artistic expression and innovation.

Artistic expression is a fundamental human need, and music is a medium through which we can communicate and convey our deepest emotions and thoughts. Whether it's through singing, playing an instrument, or composing, music allows us to express ourselves in ways that words alone cannot. It provides a unique outlet for self-discovery and self-expression, enabling us to connect with others on a profound level.

Furthermore, music has the ability to spark innovation and creativity across various fields. Many artists, writers, and inventors have found inspiration in music, using its rhythms, harmonies, and melodies to fuel their imaginations. The interplay between music and the creative process is undeniable, with countless examples of musicians who have crossed boundaries and pushed the limits of their respective art forms.

The influence of music on innovation extends beyond the realm of the arts. Numerous studies have shown that listening to music while working or studying can enhance productivity and creativity. The right choice of music can set the mood, promote focus, and unlock new perspectives. From enhancing problem-solving abilities to fostering a positive work environment, music has the power to transform our everyday activities.

In addition, music has the unique ability to shape our experiences and perceptions. It can evoke nostalgia, transporting us back to specific moments in our lives. It can also alter our moods, providing solace during difficult times or energizing us for a task at hand. Music has the power to uplift, heal, and inspire, making it an essential part of our daily lives.

From ancient chants to modern compositions, music has evolved alongside human civilization, continuously shaping and enriching our cultural heritage. Its role in artistic expression and innovation cannot be overstated. Music transcends language barriers, connects diverse communities, and has the capacity to evoke emotions and ignite creativity in every one of us. So, whether you're a musician, an artist, or someone who simply appreciates the power of melodies, embrace the profound effects of music and let it enhance your everyday experiences.

Using Music to Overcome Creative Blocks

In our fast-paced, demanding world, it is not uncommon to experience creative blocks. Whether you are an artist, writer, or simply someone who enjoys expressing themselves creatively, these blocks can be frustrating and discouraging. However, there is a powerful tool that can help you overcome these obstacles and tap into your creative potential: music.

Music has a profound effect on our everyday experiences. It has the ability to evoke emotions, transport us to different places and times, and even alter our mood. But its influence goes beyond mere entertainment. Music has the power to unlock our creativity and help us break through creative blocks.

One of the ways music can aid in overcoming creative blocks is by providing a distraction from the problem at hand. When we are stuck on a creative project, our mind becomes fixated on the issue, making it difficult to come up with new ideas. By listening to music, we shift our focus away from the problem, allowing our subconscious mind to work on finding a solution. The melodies and rhythms can create a sense of flow, enabling our thoughts to flow freely and generate fresh ideas.

Furthermore, music can also serve as a source of inspiration. Different genres and styles of music evoke different feelings and emotions. By curating a playlist that resonates with the mood or theme of your creative project, you can tap into the emotions that will fuel your creativity. For example, if you are working on a writing piece that requires a sense of adventure, listening to epic orchestral music or cheerful folk tunes may help ignite your imagination and set the tone for your work.

In addition to acting as a distraction and a source of inspiration, music can also improve our focus and concentration. Research has shown that listening to certain types of music, such as classical or instrumental pieces, can enhance cognitive abilities and increase productivity. This enhanced focus can be especially beneficial when we are facing creative blocks, as it allows us to delve deeper into our thoughts and ideas.

In conclusion, music has the power to influence every aspect of our lives, including our creative endeavors. By using music as a tool to overcome creative blocks, we can tap into our creative potential and unleash our imagination. Whether we need a distraction, inspiration, or improved focus, music can be a powerful ally on our creative journey. So the next time you find yourself facing a creative block, turn up the volume, let the melodies guide you, and watch as your creativity soars to new heights.

Chapter 9: Music and Education

The Benefits of Music Education

Music has always had a profound impact on our everyday lives, influencing our moods, emotions, and even our behavior. But did you know that music education can have wide-ranging benefits beyond just the pleasure of listening to a catchy tune? In this subchapter, we will explore the numerous advantages that music education offers to everyone, regardless of age or background.

One of the most remarkable benefits of music education is its positive effect on cognitive development. Numerous studies have shown that learning to play a musical instrument can enhance memory, attention, and problem-solving skills. The complex nature of music stimulates various areas of the brain, promoting improved brain function and mental agility. Children who engage in music education typically perform better in other academic subjects, as music fosters discipline, creativity, and critical thinking abilities.

Moreover, music education has been found to enhance emotional well-being. Playing an instrument or participating in a choir provides an outlet for self-expression, enabling individuals to channel their emotions in a healthy and constructive manner. This can be particularly beneficial for children and adolescents who may struggle with emotional regulation. Music education can boost self-esteem, reduce anxiety and depression, and improve overall mental health.

In addition, music education fosters social skills and promotes teamwork. Group music lessons or ensemble performances require collaboration, cooperation, and communication among participants. Students learn to listen to one another, follow cues, and synchronize their efforts, developing essential skills for effective teamwork. Music education provides a platform for individuals to connect with like-minded people, building friendships and a sense of belonging.

Furthermore, music education nurtures cultural appreciation and global awareness. By exploring various musical genres and styles from different cultures, individuals gain a deeper understanding and respect for diversity. Music has the power to transcend language barriers, connecting people from different backgrounds and fostering cross-cultural dialogue.

Whether you are a student, a parent, or an adult seeking personal enrichment, music education offers countless benefits. From enhancing cognitive abilities to promoting emotional well-being, fostering social skills, and nurturing cultural appreciation, the impact of music education is far-reaching and profound. So why wait? Embrace the transformative power of music education and unlock a world of possibilities.

Music as a Tool for Learning and Retention

In our daily lives, music has an uncanny ability to enhance and impact various aspects of our existence. From entertainment to relaxation, music has proven to be an influential force that resonates with people from all walks of life. However, its power extends far beyond mere enjoyment; music has a profound effect on our ability to learn and retain information. In this subchapter, we will explore why music impacts everything we do and how it can be utilized as a valuable tool for learning and retention.

Music has a unique way of engaging our brains and emotions simultaneously. Research has shown that listening to music activates multiple regions of the brain, including those responsible for memory, attention, and language processing. This activation creates a neural network that strengthens our cognitive abilities, making it easier for us to absorb and retain information.

One of the most significant benefits of using music as a learning tool is its ability to enhance focus and concentration. Certain types of music, such as classical or instrumental compositions, have been proven to improve attention span and reduce distractions. By incorporating music into our study or work routines, we can create an environment that promotes productivity and efficient learning.

Moreover, music can also serve as a mnemonic device, aiding in the retention of information. When we associate specific information with a melody or rhythm, it becomes easier to recall that information later on. This technique has been utilized by many students to memorize formulas, historical events, or foreign language vocabulary. By harnessing the power of music, we can transform our learning experience into a more enjoyable and fruitful endeavor.

Another fascinating aspect of music's impact on learning is its influence on our emotions and mood. Listening to uplifting or calming music can create a positive emotional state, reducing stress and anxiety. This emotional well-being enhances our cognitive abilities, allowing us to think more clearly and effectively process information.

In conclusion, music holds a significant place in our everyday lives, and its impact on learning and retention should not be underestimated. Whether we are studying for exams, absorbing new information at work, or simply trying to remember something important, music can serve as a valuable tool to enhance our cognitive abilities. By incorporating music into our learning routines, we can enjoy the benefits of increased focus, improved memory, and enhanced emotional well-being. So, let us embrace the power of melodies and harness their potential to make learning an enriching and fulfilling experience.

Incorporating Music into Different Learning Environments

Music has a profound impact on our everyday experiences, and its influence extends far beyond our entertainment and leisure activities. In fact, music has the power to enhance various learning environments, enabling individuals to absorb information more effectively and engage in a deeper understanding of the subject matter. Whether you are a student, a teacher, or a lifelong learner, incorporating music into your learning environment can have numerous benefits that extend well beyond the realm of music itself.

One of the primary reasons why music enhances learning is its ability to stimulate multiple areas of the brain simultaneously. Research has shown that when we listen to music, various regions of the brain responsible for memory, attention, and creativity are activated. This heightened brain activity enhances our cognitive abilities, making it easier to absorb and retain information. For this reason, educators and trainers have begun incorporating background music into their classrooms and training sessions to improve focus and concentration.

Moreover, music has the power to evoke emotions and create a positive learning environment. When we listen to music that resonates with us, our mood improves, stress levels decrease, and we become more receptive to new ideas and concepts. This emotional connection to music can be harnessed in the learning environment to create a positive and conducive atmosphere for effective learning. By playing soothing music during study sessions or incorporating catchy tunes into educational materials, educators can make the learning experience more enjoyable and engaging for students of all ages.

Additionally, music can be used as a mnemonic device to aid in information retention. Have you ever found yourself effortlessly remembering the lyrics to a song you heard years ago? This phenomenon is known as the "music effect" and is based on the idea that our brains are wired to remember information presented in a musical format. By integrating music into learning materials, such as creating educational songs or using melodic patterns to memorize important facts, learners can improve their recall and retention of information.

In conclusion, music has a profound impact on every aspect of our lives, including the way we learn. By incorporating music into different learning environments, we can tap into its powerful effects on our cognitive abilities, emotional state, and memory. Whether you are a student seeking to improve your academic performance or a teacher looking for innovative teaching techniques, music can be a valuable tool in enhancing the learning experience. So, embrace the power of melodies and let music guide you towards a more enriching and effective learning journey.

Chapter 10: Conclusion: Harnessing the Power of Music in Everyday Life

Reflecting on the Profound Effects of Music

Music is a universal language that transcends barriers and speaks to the depths of our souls. It has the power to evoke emotions, trigger memories, and influence our behavior. From the moment we wake up to the time we go to bed, music is intertwined with our everyday experiences. In this subchapter, we will explore the profound effects of music and understand why it has the ability to touch every aspect of our lives.

Music has the remarkable ability to alter our moods and emotions. Have you ever noticed how a sad song can bring tears to your eyes or a joyful tune can make you want to dance? This is because music activates the reward centers in our brains, releasing dopamine, a natural feel-good chemical. Whether we need a pick-me-up or a moment of solace, music provides us with the emotional outlet we seek.

Furthermore, music has been shown to enhance cognitive abilities. Numerous studies have demonstrated that listening to music can improve focus, memory, and problem-solving skills. It stimulates different parts of our brain, promoting neural connections and boosting overall cognitive function. This is why many individuals find it easier to concentrate on tasks or find inspiration while listening to their favorite tunes.

The impact of music goes beyond our emotional and cognitive states. It also plays a significant role in our social interactions. Think about how music brings people together at concerts, parties, or even during a casual gathering with friends. It creates a sense of unity and shared experiences, fostering connections and deepening relationships. Music has the power to break down barriers and create a sense of belonging, irrespective of cultural backgrounds or language barriers.

Moreover, music can influence our behavior and even shape our identities. It has the ability to transport us to different time periods, cultures, and even alter our perception of reality. Whether it's a protest song inspiring a movement for change or a lullaby soothing a restless child, music has the power to change the course of history and impact our personal lives in profound ways.

In conclusion, music matters because it affects every aspect of our lives. Its ability to evoke emotions, enhance cognition, foster social connections, and shape our behaviors is unparalleled. Whether you are a casual listener or a devoted music enthusiast, take a moment to reflect on the profound effects music has on your everyday experiences. Embrace the melodies, rhythms, and lyrics that have the power to transform your world.

Practical Strategies for Integrating Music into Daily Routines

In the fast-paced world we live in, it is easy to overlook the profound impact that music has on our everyday experiences. From the moment we wake up to the time we go to bed, music has the power to enhance and elevate every aspect of our lives. This subchapter aims to provide practical strategies for integrating music into our daily routines, allowing us to fully harness its transformative effects.

1. Energize Your Mornings: Start your day off on a high note by creating a playlist of uplifting and energizing tunes. Whether it's a catchy pop song or an upbeat classical piece, let the music set the tone for a productive and positive day ahead.

2. Elevate Your Workouts: Music has been shown to boost motivation and enhance physical performance. Create a playlist of fast-paced songs that inspire you to push harder during your workouts. The rhythm and energy of the music will keep you motivated and help you achieve your fitness goals.

3. Enhance Daily Chores: Turn mundane tasks into enjoyable experiences by incorporating music into your daily chores. Whether you're doing laundry, cooking, or cleaning, choose music that matches the tempo of the task at hand. Not only will this make the chores more enjoyable, but it will also help you stay focused and efficient.

4. Create a Relaxing Evening Ritual: Wind down after a long day with calming music that promotes relaxation and tranquility. Whether it's classical, jazz, or ambient music, allow the melodies to soothe your mind and help you unwind before bedtime.

5. Boost Productivity: During focused work or study sessions, instrumental music without lyrics can help improve concentration and enhance productivity. Create a playlist of instrumental tracks that keep you engaged and focused on the task at hand.

6. Foster Connection: Use music as a tool to connect with loved ones. Whether it's singing together, playing instruments, or simply sharing favorite songs, music can strengthen relationships and create lasting memories.

By integrating music into our daily routines, we tap into its profound effects on our emotions, productivity, and overall well-being. So, why wait? Start incorporating music into your everyday life and experience the transformative power it has to offer. Let the melodies shape your moods, enhance your experiences, and bring joy to every aspect of your life.

Remember, music matters, and it has the ability to enhance everything we do.

The Enduring Influence of Melodies on Our Everyday Experiences

Music has an astonishing power to influence and shape our daily lives in ways we may not even realize. From the moment we wake up to the soothing tunes of our alarm clocks, to the melodies that accompany us throughout the day, music has an undeniable impact on our emotions, productivity, and overall well-being. In this subchapter, we will explore the profound effects of melodies on our everyday experiences, delving into why music influences everything we do.

One of the most remarkable aspects of music is its ability to evoke emotions within us. Whether it's the upbeat tempo of a pop song that instantly lifts our spirits or the haunting melody of a melancholic ballad that brings tears to our eyes, music has the power to tap into our deepest emotions. It can transport us to a different time and place, triggering memories and reminding us of significant moments in our lives. From celebrations to heartbreaks, music becomes intertwined with our experiences, shaping our emotions and allowing us to express ourselves in ways words alone cannot.

Moreover, music has the ability to affect our productivity and performance. Numerous studies have shown that certain types of music can enhance concentration, creativity, and cognitive abilities. For instance, listening to classical music while studying or working has been found to increase focus and improve memory retention. On the other hand, energetic and upbeat tunes can boost motivation during exercise or mundane tasks, making them more enjoyable and helping us push through to the end.

Beyond emotions and productivity, music also plays a significant role in social interactions and cultural experiences. Whether it's a shared love for a particular genre or attending a live concert, music has the power to bring people together, fostering connections and creating a sense of community. It serves as a universal language that transcends borders and unites individuals from diverse backgrounds, allowing for shared experiences and a deeper understanding of one another.

In conclusion, the enduring influence of melodies on our everyday experiences is undeniable. From impacting our emotions and productivity to fostering connections and enhancing cultural experiences, music plays a central role in our lives. It has the power to uplift, inspire, and shape our moods, actions, and interactions. So, the next time you find yourself humming a tune or tapping your foot to the rhythm, remember that music is not just a background noise but an integral part of the human experience—a force that influences everything we do.